COME DOWN WOOD

A YEAR IN THE LIFE OF
A DALES WOODLAND

Words and pictures by Judith Bromley

with additional paintings by Robert Nicholls

GREAT NORTHERN

GREAT NORTHERN

Midland Chambers, 1 Wells Road, Ilkley, LS29 9JB

© Judith Bromley 2003

ISBN (Hardback): 0-9544002-3-2

ISBN 0-9544002-4-0

Printed by

The Amadeus Press, Bradford

British Cataloguing in Publication Data

A catalogue for this book is available in the British Library

Contents

Acknowledgements

For Nik, Robert Nicholls, to celebrate many years of marriage and partnership, of countless magic walks through innumerable woods and forests; thank you for enriching this book with your beautiful illustrations of animals and birds.

A very special thanks to the Scarr family, and in memory of the older generation, who allowed me to visit and get to know their wood almost as well as they do.

I am especially grateful to David Bellamy for writing the inspiring Foreword.

Thank you to all my family and friends who have supported me throughout this venture; and also to all of you who are passionate, as I am, about our natural Dales environment, and who love and care for our whole planet. It is in learning about the little things that are close to us that we gain more understanding of the intricacy and complexity of the whole.

Foreword

"Come Down to the Wood"

Having read Judith's book and enjoyed her pictures I too want to go down to that wood. Though tempted I now never will and thereby hangs my tale…

When I was a child, there were many more such woods scattered across the countryside, even around London. Real wild woods where Mother Nature had been holding her sylvan breath for more than 5000 years. Indeed it was in one such wood in Surrey that I found my road to Damascus.

Over the millennia people used those woods, hunting and gathering, removing trees for many purposes even coppicing large areas. Fortunately for us they had not destroyed their community of native plants and animals, nor their sanctity of purpose.

Each one had stood the test of time and climatic change, binding the good earth onto the bedrock from which they had helped it form and had kept it in good heart. The organic soil and native forest together providing cool shade in summer and protection from the winds and snows of winter. They too hold back the floods when wet and trickle feed the springs when dry. Together they provide a myriad of habitats, a living cathedral of hope for all our futures.

Farming families of our Neolithic past, their descendants and incomers alike, all in need of food opened up much of the land. Destroying the continuity of woodland cover with axes of stone, bronze and iron that created a new diversity of landscape and habitat: grassland, meadow, pasture, moor and heath. As the population grew so the wild wood shrank, linked at first through the craftmansmanship of people who laid the hedgerows each in due season.

So it was that England's multicoloured and pleasant land with distant vistas and views, as I knew it as a child, came into being, bursting with what we now call biodiversity. Sadly the past 60 years has, thanks to the common agricultural policy been catastrophic in landscape, wildflower and wildlife terms and many of those woodland cathedrals have disappeared from the face of our land.

This wonderful book tells the story of one such wildwood that still nestles in a northern dale, a story of stability through constant change, season by season, sunrise to sunset and around the clock again.

It is a treasure to be kept in your library and read with hope again and again.

Hope, because clear across this realm and the world people of every colour, creed, calling and kind, realising that they have lost so much their parents and grandparents took for granted, are taking part in what I like to call the green renaissance. Working in partnership they are beginning to stitch their patch back into more natural working order.

So why won't I go to see this particular wood? Well this wood has no path and in the knowledge that too many tramping feet can cause enormous damage I will leave that privilege to local caring people.

People who, like Judith are already part of the green renaissance will, with care, put more woods like this back into place across the hills and dales of this land that will once again be, for ever England. Indeed I will be part of it for when my time has come I have, thanks to the Arbory Trust chosen a woodland burial, I will become a tree and live another allotted span in a sylvan heaven here on earth.

Thank you for caring

David Bellamy, Bedburn 2003

'COME DOWN TO THE WOOD'

I am privileged to have been able to visit this wood for at least a decade, spending many hours walking, painting, drawing, or simply sitting here, being here.

I decided to put my work together into a study of the wild flowers through the seasons, but the sheer enormity of the task began to overwhelm me. Not just the flowers were calling for my attention, but also the trees, the wildlife - birds, animals, insects, ferns and fungi.

As time went on, rather than being a documentation of the wild life, it became a portrait of the spirit of the place, and my relationship with it. I have been helped greatly by the addition of Robert's paintings of animals and birds .

The wood is hidden away in a little valley of its own. It runs from west to east so, from the main dale below, all that can be seen is a row of trees along the crest of a hill. I like to climb up from the farm through the pasture, High Close, and a meadow, Hardraw Bank, to enter through a stile at the southern edge. During the walk I often turn to look behind me to watch the landscape spreading out - updale, downdale, and across to the distinctive silhouettes of the fells opposite.

There is no public footpath. I come here past the rambling mullion windowed old
farmhouse with permission from the family, who love their wood as I do.
It pleases us, through this book, to be able to share it, and its secrets, with you.
We hope you will find enjoyment within these pages; and also that you may come
to treasure even more deeply the rhythm of the seasons in all woodland places,
many of which are under threat from our rapidly developing 'civilisation'.

I have written in the first person so that you may imagine that you are
walking, seeing, finding, exploring the wood yourself.

My dog, a farm bred short-haired collie, comes with us through this book.
She was born mainly white out of a litter expected to be black, so we called her
Daisy - Dog Daisy.

So, come, across the farmyard and up High Close

to the top of the hill.....

through the stone stile and..

down to the wood......

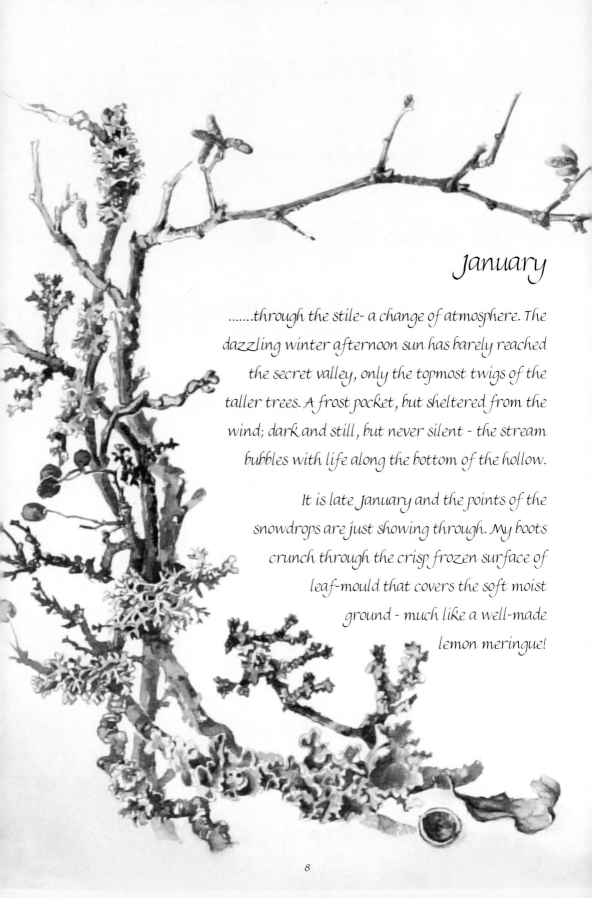

January

.......through the stile- a change of atmosphere. The dazzling winter afternoon sun has barely reached the secret valley, only the topmost twigs of the taller trees. A frost pocket, but sheltered from the wind; dark and still, but never silent - the stream bubbles with life along the bottom of the hollow.

It is late January and the points of the snowdrops are just showing through. My boots crunch through the crisp frozen surface of leaf-mould that covers the soft moist ground - much like a well-made lemon meringue!

I like to turn to my right and walk along a flat open area, and then double back to the stream after creeping through a thicket of blackthorn. Encrusted as they are with lichens, I have to look very closely at the sloe twigs to find the tight tiny round flower buds clustered at the tips - not dead after all.

Also, apparently choked by the winter's growth of lichen, dormant hazel catkins stick out at all angles waiting for warmer weather. First to show signs of green life is always the honeysuckle - soft rounded leaves brave the worst that winter sends, as it twists and climbs its way up the trees and shrubs to reach the light.

Sometimes I can cross over here at this eastern end, if the water is not in spate, and then scramble up and walk back west along the tangled 'wild side'.

Although mostly a deciduous wood, there are a number of ancient holly trees, looking their best now in the winter months. Near one of them, on a bed of moss, I find a scattering of hazelnut shells, cracked open by a squirrel hungrily digging into his savings. I've learned that a woodmouse will 'chiggle' holes in nuts; you can see the toothmarks radiating around the hole. A squirrel will break them open, that is if she can find where she buried her stores.

A scattering of downy white pigeon feathers tells of a hawk strike. Up by the top wall I find what is perhaps a foxy story, the skeleton of a rabbit is spread about - its death providing dinner for another life.

Tree trunks are covered with amazing bright green moss and dead bracken still hangs, taller than me, on outstretched branches. In some places the bark has been stripped by rabbits or deer whilst the nourishment they find in the undergrowth was covered by deep snow.

A wild rose has climbed up one of the larger trees bearing its vermilion hips high into the sky. Underneath, scraps of the orange fruits litter the ground betraying where the birds have feasted, dropping their crumbs amongst the dead leaves, moss and twigs.

We make our way back down the slope to where larches and pines grow gracefully tall together. A plantation within the wood, it has quite a different mood. Here there is no ground cover except for many seasons' depth of needles, which spring gently under my silent tread. Fresh rabbit burrowings have exposed sprouting bluebell bulbs from deep below.

A little further on I can cross back over the water. My dog cheekily bounces past, knocking me off balance as I teeter over the slippery stones.

After taking a quick look at a hole high in an ash tree to see if the owl's nest is occupied, I clamber up the opposite bank to the top stile, and out into a field called Huncher Ellers, Ellers being an old name for meadowland.

I emerge from the wood just in time to see the golden glow of sunset behind a crisp horizon of deep indigo hills. Looking behind me, over the tree-tops, the last rays cast a deep pink light onto the limestone crags.

STIRRING

February

Torrents of rain have caused the
main river to burst its banks.
At times it has looked as though
someone has put a plug in the dale
somewhere, causing it to gradually
fill up like a bath. But all those
dismal soaking wet days
have been followed by a clean
drying wind.

Today is one of those rare delicious
February mornings - blue sky,
slanting sun - mild with a promise
of more warmth to come.
Leaving the floods down
below, I approach the wood.
Tree trunks glow a brilliant
mossy green, and crisp blue shadows race
over the landscape as the wind pushes white
billowing clouds from west to east.

Snowdrops are the first flowers of the year to appear. The struggle to thrust up through frozen earth and blanket of snow is over, and their cool white presences stand slim in the dank leaf mould. Following not far behind are the bluebell shoots and tiny crinkled primrose leaves. One of the family down at the farm tells me that the earliest primrose she's ever found was one January 25... but I've never seen one as early as that. Today the green on the woodland floor is still mainly due to a fresh winter's growth of mosses - creeping over absolutely everything - stones, mud, fallen branches, and up into the trees. Where the sun has reached over the edge of the valley to the hazels, last month's stubby catkins have swelled, opened out, and dropped. They are now recognisable as the familiar lambs-tails - heralds of spring - shaking their yellow pollen into the wind.

A reddish haze over the treetops is caused by the bronze and coppery colour of millions of buds, the leaves secretly developing within their protective sheaths. As we cross the glade we disturb a little owl, all head and wings.

I can see the remains of a pigeon's nest in the bird cherry. Will it be rebuilt soon?

March

Last time I came it was a battle to get here against gale force winds. February, true to form, was 'fill-dyke' and March came in 'like a lion'. But last night there was a frost again, and a powdering of snow on the tops. The sky now is clear from horizon to horizon, a welcome respite from all the wind and rain.

The rooks seem busier, clamouring around in their tall sycamores. As I climb the hill a flock of gulls lifts from the high field they've been feeding on and circles lazily, their smart white and black uniforms impeccable, glinting in the sun. We know when March is here by the arrival of these black-headed gulls. They come to nest and breed on the moorland tarns - tempted here by rich pickings in the lambing fields. Nowadays though, the sheep give birth indoors, so the afterbirths are not generally to be found scattered over the pastures as they used to be.

Today, having entered through
the stile, I turn left to walk all the way up
the stream, over a fallen wall, to the far end of
the wood. There is an orchard of damsons here, like a
punctuation mark at the top of the wood, before the high
fields spread out into the open fell. Wild raspberry canes grow along the
wall, and nettles - a sign of human habitation- even though, so I've been
told, the barn has never been a dwelling.

The water comes down from the fellside and runs deep into a cleft that it has
worn through a limestone outcrop. Ivy clambers and cascades over the rockface,
and very old larches grow twisted, but tall, at either side. They call this the
Fairy Wood - no-one can remember why...

Heavy water has moved huge rocks about in the bed of the stream. I'm surprised
that the gales haven't wreaked more havoc amongst the trees, but the little
valley gives shelter from the worst of the weather. Dead or weak branches have
been wrenched off and cast aside, and a whole hazel bush is lying across my
path. It appears to be having a last fling, as though it was still standing - in tune
with its neighbours it is hung with catkins, both the male lambs-tails and the
tiny red female spurts.

The birds are getting busier: showing off, pairing up, and claiming territory.
Amongst the spiky twigs and red buds of a hawthorn thicket, I'm thrilled to see
a pair of long-tailed tits flirting together, their chests blushing pink
with spring colour.

The sun rises a little higher every day, and reaches down further into this hidden place. In response to its warmth an almost perceptible moving and stirring is taking place. Tiny leaves, folded, pleated, crumpled, spiralled, swell out of hard protective sheaths. Buds are bursting and shoots are sprouting.

Up at the south west corner grow some huge ancient willows whose trunks have fallen outwards with age. High up in the sky the first 'pussy' catkins shine silver against the blue. Walking back downstream, I slip about on the soft soil and fresh garlic leaves. Dog's mercury sends up curled fronds, and the angled sunlight picks out the tips of bluebell shoots. It is impossible not to tread on them here under the silver birches, although I know that tramping boots may kill the delicate plants.

On the topmost twig above me, a bullfinch sings as though his rosy breast would burst with the pleasure of it all.

My attention is drawn towards the larch and fir plantation, and there, in the dappled light, a couple of roe deer stand, watching the dog intently. They seem to know they are safe at the other side of the beck, but, as I reach for the camera, they turn and disappear silently into the undergrowth.

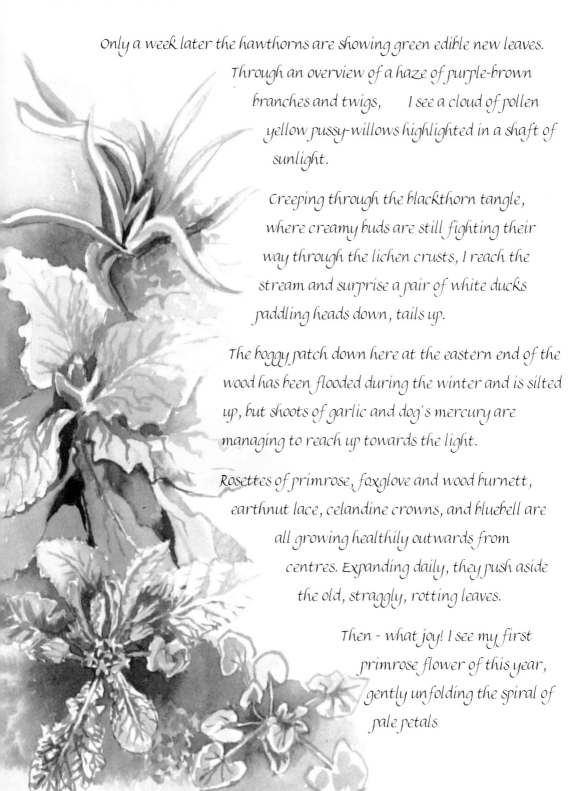

Mid March

Only a week later the hawthorns are showing green edible new leaves. Through an overview of a haze of purple-brown branches and twigs,   I see a cloud of pollen yellow pussy-willows highlighted in a shaft of sunlight.

Creeping through the blackthorn tangle, where creamy buds are still fighting their way through the lichen crusts, I reach the stream and surprise a pair of white ducks paddling heads down, tails up.

The boggy patch down here at the eastern end of the wood has been flooded during the winter and is silted up, but shoots of garlic and dog's mercury are managing to reach up towards the light.

Rosettes of primrose, foxglove and wood burnett, earthnut lace, celandine crowns, and bluebell are all growing healthily outwards from centres. Expanding daily, they push aside the old, straggly, rotting leaves.

Then - what joy! I see my first primrose flower of this year, gently unfolding the spiral of pale petals

The daffodils have thrown aside their dry papery wrappings
and their bright heads are nodding in the wind.

As we cross the clearing, my dog - head down
every rabbit hole - misses seeing...

...... a huge hare.

It leaps away over the vigorous new grass

blades that are rapidly obliterating

last year's bleached-out straws.

Hazel catkins, job done, pollen all gone, turn dry and brown, and fall. Carefully pleated fresh green leaves take their place, protecting the secret swelling of fertilised female flowers. Here, down a damp bank, the coltsfoot flower before their leaves emerge. In amongst the roots of a fallen tree the squirrels have hidden a cache of nuts with which to break their fast.

A loud hollow noise echoes around us. At first I think it is the creaking of a dead branch in the wind. When it sounds again I manage to locate it, and see a great spotted woodpecker drumming for grubs at the trunk of a large dead elm.

The birds are tuning up for spring, chattering and piping everywhere, and loudest of all, a thrush is repeating each phrase as if to try it out. A pair of young ash trees, roots in the stream, entwine together in a lifelong embrace, blending their trunks as one.

April

Swaledale sheep and lambs are gathered
around the stile as we approach. The ewes
stamp their feet and make quiet warning noises
with gentle concern for their tiny new-born lambs,
tight curls drying in the sun.

My young dog is used to taking care and not causing fright when close to
livestock. She is so glad to be out and running free on such a day, but for now
she controls her exuberance and enthusiasm. Warily, but without moving, they
allow us to pass by, standing protectively in front of their diminutive
scraps of new life.

Down we go into the little peaceful valley. Here, out of the wind, I can feel the
strength of the sun. Again we startle the big hare, who lollops almost lazily
across the flat open glade. He knows the dog couldn't muster the speed to catch
him up, and she knows I'd call her back if she tried.

The trees have pink and green haloes around them, caused by innumerable
swelling and bursting buds. The ground flora has to develop quickly now before
the leaf canopy shades it.

Armies of bluebell and ramson spears, with dog's mercury uncurling, stand
sturdy and erect under the trees. The daffodil clump near the stream spreads
out a little wider every year, but right now they are looking somewhat battered.
Have they been eaten away by the little red brown beetles who appear
to live in the yellow pollen trumpets...or is it the slugs who are to
blame? The primroses are still struggling to get started. This weather
will soon get them going if it lasts.

On the north side, which gets full sun for most of the day, the plants are much further forward. There is a warm smell of bracken and growing things. Occasional cups of celandines shine back at the sun. Under the holly trees, bright berries and a ladybird lie on a deep forest of moss, through which grow tiny holly seedlings and purple leaves of bugle. A small black slug steadily munches its way through the lot!

The wood is a haven of birdsong - tits, finches, blackbirds and thrushes... The chaffinches glow with almost tropical colour. All the birds are busy claiming territory for themselves amongst the tree tops. The clap-clap flight of a pigeon brings my attention to its nest in the bird cherry tree; and the woodpecker gives away its presence by drilling loudly.

An alder bears russet catkins on twigs still studded by black cones. Its roots, deep into the silt of the stream, come back up to the surface as striking bright orange nodules. A willow grows here too; standing with its feet in the water it bears a mass of silky pussies. Blowsy with powdery pollen, they send out a delicate perfume which attracts a great big bumble bee who lands and clambers busily over and round.

Deer slots in the soft mud mark where they came to drink. A pair of mallard fly off the water as I cross the beck to look more closely at a purple primrose - primula wanda.

I have been sitting here for a few hours now. The air is gentle and moist. I could actually see the garlic spears grow as I painted them.

The pigeon began to coo dreamily..........

Suddenly the sharp harsh sound of a pheasant, accompanied by his instantaneous wing flap, made me jump. He set up calling again and again behind me. I heard him fly over to the left, and then after a few minutes he returned and renewed his bombastic shouting... Much later, a second cock shattered the recently settled peace, calling from over to the left where the first had been. They began to shriek back and forth at each other.

Eventually the second pheasant moved back up the hill, called for the last few times, and then both fell silent- happy with each other's space.

Over an hour later, when the garlic sheaths had grown some more, a third cock started to call, much further up the wood at the other side - and so my first had to begin his challenge all over again.

Painting finished I pack up and leave them to it. I'm moving on upstream to visit the herb paris.

Up near the little gate on the northern edge the herb paris leans towards the sun. The spiral of leaves gently unfurls and they open out to make that typical formation of four, sometimes five, flat leaves. As the sun moves round, so do they, like telescope dishes, catching as much of the warmth as is possible.

How wonderful to sit here with them, feeling time and rhythm move along with the angle of the sun, seeing all the woodland plant life grow and develop as the day passes by.

Now and then the wind picks up and the cold rush of air around my back reminds me that the year is early yet.

FLOWERING

Early May

There have been many cold and turbulent April showers, but now the pasture is golden with dandelion suns. The rooks sound contented on this quiet, warm and sunny day. The ewes and lambs are at ease.

In the wood, pheasant calls punctuate a gentle
undulating chorus of birdsong, as always accompanied
by the gurgling of the gill.

As I enter I am alert for movement, and through the
tangled light and shadow I catch sight of a hind
bounding down the slope and across the beck.

A squirrel dances up a tree leaving the dog
whining and wagging on the ground.

The primroses are in full bloom. Garlic
leaves and dog's mercury now provide a
rich green carpet under the network of
tawny twigs and branches. A cloud of
white sloe blossom covers the brittle
blackthorn - even now hung with last
year's russet coloured bracken. The whole
thicket is a-buzz with bees.

I stoop to watch a fat brown furry hover-fly sip nectar from a primrose, and as I turn away I gasp out loud to see a clump of smiling violets. Heart-shaped leaves of violets, celandines, and upward pointing pyramids of wood sorrel are surrounded by pretty earthnut lace.

By mid morning the mauve-white wood sorrel flowers have lifted up their hanging heads, and now, together with the shining celandines, have opened petals wide to greet the sun. Wild strawberries' twinkling of starry flowers adds to the profusion underfoot.

The sun is warm enough for me to think of sun cream as we settle down, I to paint and the dog to watch out for me.

A waving stream of movement through the ramsons catches my eye. Keeping still and looking carefully, I'm rewarded by the sight of a red brown stoat flowing over a mossy rock in its search for prey.

Come noon, I'm clad in all my jumpers again - the sky overcast with thin cloud. Maybe this is much more appropriate for the season. Birdsong has quietened to spasmodic outbursts... and the water rushes on.

Every year I promise myself that I won't have to paint the heavily creased and veined primrose leaves again, and every year the primroses tempt me back.

In the afternoon the sun returns and I find bluebells out on a south facing bank. Below them, where it floods from time to time, succulent yellow king-cups and stubby butter-burrs are in flower. Where the soil is permanently damp, flat round platelets of golden saxifrage form a sheet of yellow green.

Now, much later on, I hear the sharp warning 'tuk-tuk' of a blackbird as I walk back towards the sloe thicket. A red admiral, which had been spread out on a warm stone, lifts up into the air. There may be a strong feeling of peace here in the wood, but having spent the day here, I know that the place is actually heaving with growing, mating, and profligating!

....a thrush sings into the evening.

Second week in May

This week's weather has been glorious and the plants seem to have packed a month's worth of growing into a few days. Always the spring gallops along too rapidly for me and I cannot work fast enough to capture the beauty of it all. I'm caught between a desire for fine enough weather to sit outside, and the wish that, when it does come, the warmth wouldn't make it all happen so quickly. A lamb is so fast asleep in the heat of the sun that even the dog's approach, investigative sniff, and my warning word, doesn't wake it.

Drifts of bluebells cover the south facing slopes, and forget-me-nots keep company with the king-cups down here where the soil is damper. Early purple orchids stand proud out of a coronet of generously spotted leaves.

After more than a decade of coming here, I know that one year there may be more of one species, whilst the next may be favoured by another. Last year, after a very wet spell, there were more primroses than I've ever seen; this time there are carpets of violets.

year by year the sun gets stronger and
harsher, but in the wood the trees
protect the ground cover at their feet. We can,
however, often get an unexpected drought
during these early months, which doesn't suit
these moisture-loving plants.

I've come across a patch of wood-sorrel with larger and more strongly coloured
mauve-pink flowers than usual. They're growing under birches whose galls hang
heavy on pendulous twigs, all of them decorated with the little sprouting green
triangular leaves.

Goldilocks and woodruff hide in less obvious corners of the wood. Bittercress is
scattered everywhere. I'm pleased to find some wood anemones in the Fairy wood,
whose beautiful larches, clad in fresh green mantles, are swaying like
waterfalls.

Here, too, there are false oxlips growing alongside primroses and cowslips - the
result of their cross fertilization. Up in the top corner the damsons are in bloom,
and there is a smaller and later flowering variety of pussy willow. I push my face
into the myriad of soft little pollen bursts and breathe in their delicate scent.
Herb-paris is fully open now; the same height, and blending perfectly with dog's
mercury and campion leaves - difficult to see if you don't know where to look.

The deer are perfectly camouflaged in amongst purplish brown trunks and twigs;
they flit soundlessly, slim and agile amongst the shadows, and we quietly veer
away, respecting this thicket as being theirs.

The birds are busy, but still have time to sing and sing endlessly into the morning
sun. Wood pigeons add a melodious soothing tone behind the burblings and
chatterings, with a thrush putting in the main tune. He repeats each line as if to
make sure we heard it.

The peace seeps into my soul, removing all the worries and frictions of daily life.
Here I can sit and simply BE- surrounded by sheer....existence!

I've been sitting very still, concentrating on my work. From the corner of my eye I noticed a tiny movement. There is a small spider spinning away, completing a web that is strung between my leg and a bluebell. Little pink and orange outer husks of leaf buds fall gently on my head and shoulders, from the sycamore above.

A great wind suddenly blows up. The dog starts from sleep, immediately alert. We are not touched by it in this hidden valley, but the treetops that reach up to the surrounding pastures sway and bend noisily. We walk over to watch as it shakes the blossom off the massive wild cherry that grows on the south bank, the petals swirl and fall. The cherry has a great presence, standing as tall as its neighbouring ash trees. Having admired it, and marvelled at its size, I then find, in complete contrast, a ground covering of moschatels - minute 'town hall clocks'.

An owl hoots, out of time, and I'm reminded that my time is running out. After these days of sun and stillness, rain and maybe snow is forecast for tomorrow.

Mid May

The weather forecast was correct. Since I last came we have had snow and overnight ground frosts. The sycamore's rosy buds have burst into red tinted leaves that are turning green as they broaden out. Amongst them the rookery sounds busy, as single birds fly backwards and forwards with purpose, collecting and delivering food to their young. The oaks that stand here with the sycamores have developed a green haze of bursting buds. The pasture of dandelions is less brilliant - the first flowers have ripened to gossamer spheres. I have to take care where I step when walking through High Close now - the cows have been turned out to grass!

Daisy Dog gets so exited when she realises where we're going, but once in the wood she doesn't roam far, preferring to stop when I stop, then go and explore ahead of me when I'm ready to move on.

The primroses are still flowering on and on, the clumps getting larger and more blowsy as spring progresses towards summer; but now the bluebells have taken over: sheets, drifts, carpets, banks of bluebells. Each season lasts much longer than I expect because the full sun on the south-facing slope gives everything a head start, then it is followed weeks later by the shaded growths on the opposite banks which look to the north.

Now the tree leaves are unfolding, the race against time has begun in earnest. In a single day the blue haze develops, I can see the bluebells rise from their leaves and open. Rowan, birch, and bird cherry are greening up nicely, although the ash trees still stand stark and bare with not a sign of life.

Stitchwort and early garlic flowers scatter white stars amongst the lush green. Shy speedwell, forget-me-nots, and bold bugle join the violets in a continuation of the bluebells' theme of blue.

In the open area grows a perfectly shaped conical bird cherry tree. Today it is in full bloom... what a sight!

It is a damp and scrunchy experience walking amongst the garlic and bluebell leaves - full of slippery, slimy sap. I try to avoid treading on the bluebells, but it is difficult. Many of the ramson flowers remain tightly wrapped, waiting erect for the signal to open safely. Much larger sheaths of wild arum also stand patiently, amongst shield shaped leaves, until warmer weather. Now here's a plant with a multitude of common names - very descriptive of its demeanour too. Among the less erotic and more repeatable local names are: lords and ladies, cuckoo pint, and parson in the pulpit.

Stepping quietly past the goose-grass... I don't know which of us jumps first, myself, or the leveret ambling towards me. I stand stock-still and he grunts a little warning as he turns off to the left into the undergrowth. The path opens out just past here and there's evidence that this dry flat space is used as a dust-bath by pheasants.

The blackthorn thicket has undergone a change. No longer decorated with white blossom, it is now misty green with tiny leaves. I will not know until later in the year if the fruit had time to set before being damaged by the frost - it has caught the tips of some of the bracken and fern fronds.

The skeleton of a stoat screaming the agony of a winter death now lies on a bed of violets in the dewy grass. Milkmaids, fresh in the green valley bottom, open fragile petals held high by tough wiry stems. Bracken unfurls, like little people with arms joyfully outstretched, celebrating resurrection. Coming up, at first with bowed heads, are water avens and ground nut, buds tightly curled below arched necks.

Down under the firs the sound is muffled and there's a different smell and feel to the air. I find small pink purslane with shiny leaves growing where nothing else can, out of the deep bed of needles.

Further along, in the fairy wood, my dog shows me a pheasant's nest at the base of one of the larches. It has ten cold eggs in it so far. The hen will return and lay some more before starting to incubate them. Where the coltsfoot were, are now flat felt-like leaves with cotton backs. Then my gaze is taken by a whole stand of early purple orchids under a greening hawthorn bush.

Third week in May

The sycamores are in full leaf now, and hanging with pendulous warm-green flowers. The sheep and lambs have been moved to the high pastures to allow the meadows to grow for grass. Amongst the dandelion clocks in Corn Close a cow stands with her new born calf. She has not been with the herd of milk cows, as they wander out to graze, and meander back in, twice daily to be milked. She has led a quieter life and this morning gave birth. Her sturdy black bull-calf knows where to nuzzle and, as he learns to suckle, she turns to lick him clean and dry.

The bird cherry has a short flowering season and is already past its best. As I look up at it, a long-tailed tit flies across, the morning sun shining vermilion through its fanned tail feathers. Silver-birch catkins shake brilliant pollen into the blue sky. In this part of the wood, greater stitchwort is scattered among the bluebells. At the foot of one of the birches grows a little mat of green and crimson bilberry leaves. On closer inspection I discover they are in flower.

Ash tree buds are bursting at last - their yellow green adding another colour and pattern to the spreading canopy. Now I can tell which of the trees are dead. Even some of the ones bursting with new life still cling on to old and useless branches. This prompts me to take a fresh look at my own life - are there areas in it that could do with an input of fresh energy, or am I burdened with some old habits that need discarding? The leaves of the rowan tree look like hands holding high to the universe their offering of tight wrapped flower buds. I know that my life is like that, a gift.

The wood smells delicious. The delicate scent of bluebells drifts across, overwhelming me, bringing tears of pleasure to my eyes. The sharp and savoury aroma of the crisp garlic leaves blends with warm wood, and earth, and in the sunshine my spirit expands into the essence of the day. A pair of peacock butterflies makes a stunning sight, fluttering and dancing together around the bluebells in a sunlit glade.

Brackens and ferns continue to gradually unfurl. Herb robert sends out his red stalked lacy leaves, and deep blue bugle stands robust where early purple orchids fade and weaken. Bog valerian and bitter-cress, confusingly similar, scatter over the damper ground. Broad leaves of foxglove and melancholy thistle slowly develop their size and strength ... and still the primroses and wood-sorrel flower on ... and on, getting floppy and lost now under fresher growth of the newcomers.

Time passes by as I paint - this time the goldilocks in the fairy wood! The magic is complete when I look up from my work and straight into the eyes of a hare, quietly nibbling the grass no more than two meters away. We contemplate one another and then he continues to browse.

I stretch out my hand to hold the dog, who shows more than a little interest, and the hare moves to munch a grass-blade a little further past me. I reach out my other hand for the camera, and he decides that some salad much further away might taste better!

All afternoon the deer have been travelling up and down the gill. I saw them walking down along the horizon to my left, and then a pair stepped more hurriedly to my right through the dense undergrowth.

Before making my way home, I have a careful look at the pheasant's nest - yes she's sitting now, perfectly camouflaged. I certainly wouldn't have seen her if I didn't know where to look. Daisy dog obediently keeps her distance.

As I approach the stile I notice a blackbird on the wall, strutting and posturing, beak down and the feathers above his tail fanned up into a ruff. I've never seen this behaviour before, but it is explained by the presence of his mate crouching in the undergrowth below. What a show- off!

End of May

The pasture is flattened by grazing cows. The heavy rain has left the dandelion clocks looking bedraggled, and the clover leaves are silver with dew drops. Just inside the stile, bluebells, open now right to the tips of their fleshy stems, are leaning against lime green lichen of the stone wall. Small snails climb over lush grass blades, already weighed down by last night's downpour. Hawthorns are dripping with frothy blossom. A cock pheasant crouching on the boundary wall glints copper in the early sun.

The open garlic flowers paint a milky way of stars across the southern slope, but today I've come specifically to paint the lords and ladies before they collapse. Shade loving, they send up spear-like bracts through shining shield shaped leaves. Unfurling, the bracts reveal pale flesh-pink phalluses, which blush as they age, darkening to passionate maroon before the whole erection collapses into papery debris.

To my painting I add water avens' shyly hanging heads, and bent necked buds, and then some primly pretty Queen Anne's Lace. I finish just in time, before black clouds blow up and block out the 'glishy' light.

As I work, Daisy stays alert, staring expectantly at a tangle of undergrowth where some small animal is hiding - far too clever to come out into the open whilst we're here. All will be clear for it soon; the comings and goings will resume when we have made our weary way home.

GREENING

June

The sycamores' leaves are broadening
and when I reach the wood today
I find a subtle change has
taken place. Spring has crept
imperceptibly into summer.

There is a quieter and less frenetic atmosphere.

The year is settling down to mature under the influence of longer days and warmer weather.

The lords and ladies have collapsed and, under the broad-leaved canopy, yellowing bluebell leaves lie flat and slimy. Unbelievably, in a shady north facing corner, some primroses flower yet. Bracken and ferns continue to uncurl to the very tips of their fronds, and little yellow stars of trailing St John's Wort shine where wild strawberry flowers sparkled earlier in the year.

Daisy whines and yelps as she claws and scratches, digging into an old hollow branch. I pull her back and find a hedgehog curled up very tight at the far end of the log, making itself as small and spiky as possible.

I walk around the wood welcoming new arrivals and greeting old friends. Goosegrass climbs high in the sloe thicket where some of the developing bracken is already as tall as me. I have to keep brushing the cobweb strands away from tickling my face as I push past prickly brambles and stinging nettles. A diminutive speedwell goes almost unnoticed amongst the grass whilst its relative, the germander, carpets a sunny patch with blue.

The blue of bugles and forget-me-nots is laced around with white doily plates of earthnut, bolder now it is fully open.

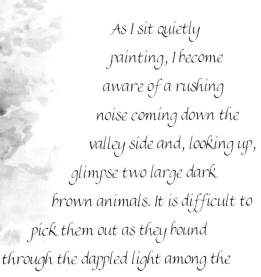

As I sit quietly painting, I become aware of a rushing noise coming down the valley side and, looking up, glimpse two large dark brown animals. It is difficult to pick them out as they bound through the dappled light among the trees. One appears to be chasing the other; they pause, and I think they've seen me. It must be the calves being frisky... they look my way as if they might come and investigate... then run off as though playing, and I realise, on seeing a white rump, that it is the deer.

After a few moments' silence I get back to work before a squeal attracts my attention again, and back they come along the valley bottom just a few yards away. The larger one with short antlers is doing the chasing and notices me and veers off up into the trees. The smaller doe comes closer, pausing quite nearby to look behind to see why the buck is no longer following. I watch spellbound before she realises my presence and runs back, not seeming to be afraid. Rather than panicking, they appear to still be having fun. Could the roe deer's rutting season be beginning early?

Bees are busy in the garlic flowers whose savoury smell reminds me that it's time to go home and cook the evening meal.

Second week in June

Today I've come to paint the bracken. It appears to be bashful and shy as it pushes out of the ground, bowed right over in a loop. Each shoot seems to be hiding its head in its hands, protectively. However, it is strong and virile, and secretly harbours a carcinogenic substance. As I paint the fronds uncurling one by one, I am reminded of human figures in a multitude of expressive postures. 'Arms' gradually spread open wide, 'head' straightens up, and the last bit to unfurl is the 'hand and fingers', the fist.

I have recently been thinking a lot about misunderstanding and how, through words and body language, we can sometimes give out and receive the wrong messages from one another. Looking at this community of bracken, each individual appears to describe different stresses and strains, each showing different reactions to adversity. I see gestures that resemble shock, self-protective aggression, modesty, beckoning, brave open arms stretched wide. Some look ready to pounce, there are grins, grimaces, and others look dragon-like with horns. The full grown plants with arms, hands and fingers outstretched, help to protect and shelter the less well developed. Some grow close together, embracing only each other.

I realise, as I paint them, what a responsibility we have - not only to care for each other in trouble - but to recognise what effect our reactions to our own inner pain can have upon others. With arms open wide we can be receptive, though vulnerable; but we cannot hold out a helping hand to others if our fists are still clenched from our own distress.

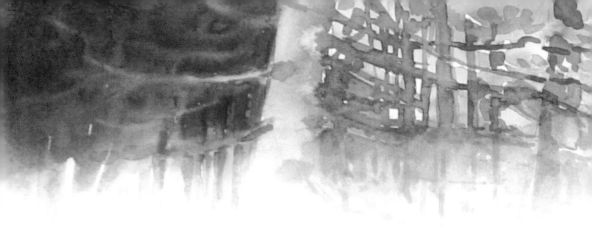

Brilliant bluebottles buzz and sun themselves. A bright orange fly visits a deep purple bugle. If the sun goes in for any length of time, or when I'm sitting in the shade, I have to take precautions against midges. I'm also in the company of slugs! A huge black slimy blob has been grazing away near my foot - making slow advances on my lunch-box.

The willow is fluffy again, this time with seed, which seems to become lighter than air as it drifts off across the glade at the slightest sigh, moving absent-mindedly in the afternoon heaviness. Caterpillars in the bird cherry have started to weave silken hammocks, folding the leaves up around them for food and protection.

Woolly aphids fur themselves up on the twigs; and as I admire the small white flowers of the holly, I find leaf miners tunnelling away in its leathery blades. From the lace-like well-eaten hazel foliage above me, a looper lowers itself on gossamer thread to my arm. It measures its way down to my hand and across my board.

Time to go before I get devoured too - but before leaving I take a look at the northside. The stream is low enough to cross and, as I scramble through the thickening undergrowth, I glimpse a slim ginger-brown body slink over the wall - was it a fox? A peep into the pheasant's nest as I pass... a tiny face is looking back at me from half an eggshell. Seeing a couple of wee chicks tottering around, and some unhatched eggs, I quickly call the dog to follow me and stay by, hoping that the other visitor hasn't got wind of what's happening here.

Later June

On a hot day in June, after a few days of rain, I anticipate midges and lather myself with anti-bite oils before adventuring out through well-cropped pastures and shining buttercup meadows. All is quiet in the sycamores as I leave the hazy blue dale to descend into the dappled shade of the ghyll. Foxgloves peer open-mouthed over the wall at the cow parsley in the meadow. The magenta bells hang from velvet stalks, graceful, tall, and strong. Dark spots, ringed with white, pour out onto fur fringed bottom lips.

The first glimpse through the stile is of green and white. The earth nut, no longer shy, predominates; but, looking closer, herb robert, speedwell, and herb bennet scatter pink, blue, and yellow confetti into the darkness of the woodland floor. The canopy, broad mature overlapping layers, cuts out the light. Unfurled ferns arch into the shade and bracken crowds throng, uncurling tips, across the glade. Water avens' hanging heads are lifted, proud with seed; vetch grows lush; and garlic's starry heads shine now with round, green, triple swellings. Woody cranesbill, seen more commonly in meadows, flowers here in its 'proper' place, with crimson campions, and amongst fine masses of stitchwort leaves - now white with cuckoo spit not blooms.

Across the open space the grasses hang heavy, and powder pollen as we pass. Pink bistort stands straight and tall, crosswort climbs and silver cinquefoil creeps. Wild rosebuds' pink-kissed crumpled petals, folded round an inner crown of sepals, respond to heat and light.

The sun's warmth is now assured, so strong I seek the shade, though that means a flighty bite or two!... which is best, bites or burns?

...And then, as though I needed more assaults, a nettle stings right through my trousers. Even the nettles have lacy leaves. Who is so keen for their young to live such a protected life that their caterpillars have developed a taste for formic acid? I know it could be red admirals or tortoiseshells, but not having gloves I don't investigate.

The common spotted orchids try to rise above the wet grass. More foxgloves tower, with bracken as tall as me, under the alders near the beck, where amber water rushes after last night's thundery torrent. Quiet now, and lethargic after the frenzy of spring, slowly and everywhere things grow higher and higher, fatter and fatter, broader and flatter.

Sycamore and ash keys hang in place of pendulous flowers. Bugles stretch ever upwards out of a sea of sorrel leaves. Huge cotton-felt umbrellas of butterbur extend ever outwards above the mossy stones. Goose-grass is knee-high and climbing, not to forget the forget-me-nots nearing the tops of wire thread stems, alternate seedpurses ripening as they go.

I cannot see across the valley now. The wood is a silent secret. Humid and still, I find it an effort just to walk along the flat, never mind to climb the northern slope. Pushing on through the undergrowth I do not know how far I've come. A stick cracks under my tread, a pheasant calls a warning, and a pigeon flights above my head.

Reaching a little clearing I can see the firs and pines below, wearing their summer plumage, and we clamber down again, passing the budding guelder rose. Daisy must stay near me when, standing in the cool air and muffled quiet of the evergreens, I hear a mallard duck calling softly to her brood of chicks.

A wagtail flits through a shaft of light towards a scattering of pink purslane. Here, in the dark, the foxglove mouths remain tightly shut; the flowers when they open will be pallid and fragile.

Crossing the stream again I notice pom-poms of sanicle growing from deep moss. It looks like a different plant altogether from the one I found earlier in the year. In this deep far corner of the wood a fallen hawthorn blocks my path. Lying with branches stretched towards the bubbling beck, it denies death by blooming still. Its falling has left a patch of sky above and sunlight reaches in where none could penetrate before.

I enter the fairy wood, its larches fully clad. Growing tall out of the soft grass stand fat buds of melancholy thistles. The raspberry canes are flowering, but the silken parcels in the bird cherry increase in size - the caterpillars stripping the leaves as they weave along. I decide not to battle against nettles to the damsons, and turn towards the willows, checking the pheasant's nest on passing to find... only eggshells!

Flies, hover-flies, butterflies, and moths dance in and out of the dappled light. Grass stems tremble as a breath of air wafts through the sultry heat. Suddenly all is excitement when a family of squirrels leap and fly high in the birches. Daisy feels cheated that she can't join in, but loves the fun of it all.

I look for the honeysuckle and wouldn't have found it if I hadn't remembered seeing the soft leaves during the winter. The persistent woody stems clamber and wind up and around a hazel who seems to be collapsing under the weight. The younger vines wave and wander, hoping to reach more support. The whole colony stretches along a row of six or more hazels and then across to an ash sapling, unchecked and invasive. Finally it embraces a small sycamore. High up, the buds nearest the light are almost opening, but down here in the gloom they are only just beginning to form. I look forward to smelling the blossoms on my next visit.

Dog Daisy has investigated every hole, scent and trail, and shown me by 'pointing' where all the inhabitants are hiding, but she cannot tell me who they are! It has been a lazy hazy mid-summer day. Just as I am about to go through the stile, past where the holly is shedding old hardened leaves in favour of new soft spiny shoots, I spy in the shadows.... can you believe it?.. three late primroses.

Early July

The dale is shimmering with heat. On the whole we had a wet June, unusually cold with spells of north wind, so some of the flowers and plants are developing later than usual.

The meadow I pass through is pink with soft grass - Yorkshire fog - waiting to be cut. The lower half of the field lies in mown stripes ready to be gathered; and the meadow below that one is scraped clean and bleached ochre. Thankfully, from time to time, a heat haze dims the fierceness of the sun. Tractors return after a brief lunch-break, dashing whilst the weather holds good.

Foxgloves tower higher and higher, a stately row of them peering over the wall at the sunny dale below. The hawthorns are adorned with wild roses, blushing pink like the meadow grass, intertwining prickly stem to barbed twig; graceful arching supported by sturdy tangle. The ash tree bears huge bunches of green keys. It seems to be only a few weeks since the ashes came into leaf; the ash is a late developer but a fast worker!

Into the wood I find the ground cover greener than ever, scattered still with speedwell, burnet and herb robert. In the flat valley bottom the common spotted orchids have grown to an amazing height, standing amongst pollen heavy grasses. Branched yellow marsh hawk's beard, and tall green dock, wave gently in a faint breeze under the dark canopy. Brambles ramble unchecked, scratching at me; and goose-grass climbs everything it can, catching at me. The earthnut is now green with seed and the campions look straggly and leggy.

Ferns are all unfurled; five foot bracken, soon to tower above me, their lower leaves outstretch hand in hand, are still uncurling the very topmost tips.

A wren is agitated as I climb into the blackthorn to inspect a purple glowing thistle head, spikes glistening in the sun. Then I spot her fledglings, so tiny and unsure, bobbing with anxiety.

The tips of the tall straight pines sway gently, shushing as water laps the shingle. An old and massive cobweb, slung between the lower branches like a fishing net, has caught only pine needles. A fresher one, a little higher up, is guarded in the centre by its creator who is getting fat on the many insects he has ensnared.

As I stand with the melancholy thistles, Daisy runs ahead and, from the furthest point of the wood, a doe leaps out into the meadow. She pauses there, elbow high in the grass, and glances back and forth, from me to where she emerged. I guess she must have a fawn concealed in the damson orchard, so we retrace our steps and leave her to return.

Later, along the soft mud of the top path, a line of tiny deer slots following a larger set shows my hunch was correct. After rutting in summer, the pregnancy lasts through the winter, and the doe gives birth in spring. This fawn will be from last year's mating.

The rowan blossom has finished and the berries are beginning to form. In place of it, the elders' wonderful summer scent drifts out from flat cream foamy plates of flowers. An elliptical view of the blossoms at the top of each tree, and a fuller view of each one lower down, they describe well the roundedness of the whole bush. I also find that its relative, the guelder rose, is flowering beautifully now. Wood woundwort sends out a completely different aroma as we push past its furry leaves - a sharp and acrid smell, but not unpleasant.

Overwhelmed by heat and height, I struggle wearily through the jungle of growth. The path is not often walked at this time of year, probably because of midges. But my heart and energy soar when I find another honeysuckle, this one in the Fairy wood and in full bloom... then I come across another and another - honeysuckles climbing every tree. The sweet scent of the pale gold flowers combines with a cooling breeze to revive and refresh me.

It is the end of a blazing hot day. I sit on a bank of sweet lady's bedstraw under the birches and watch the midges dance. A light evening breeze blows wild rose petals floating down from the great height that the climber has reached, supported as it is by the other trees. There are carpets of lush wood sorrel and healthy primrose leaves to remind me of the earlier part of the year, and yes, one single battered primrose flower struggling on in the deep shade.

We leave the wood along the top path, and on our way pass the honeysuckle that I found last month. I now know that one of the family from the farm has spent a lot of time over the years threading the vines back into the wood to stop it emerging into Huncher Ellers where it would be grazed on by the stock.

End July

It has rained a great deal this month and, where the meadow ground was ochre bare after silaging, it is now fresh green again. In the warm moist atmosphere some of the foxgloves have risen to well over six foot. Each whole spire portrays the complete development from a few remaining buds at the very tip, to mature seed-cases at the base.

The wild rose and elderflowers are gone, and the woodland green has darkened. I can see swelling hazelnuts against the thick foliage. The brambles are blooming, in amongst a tangled mass of tall nettles, spiky thistles, and graceful grasses. Maroon woundwort, and valiant herb robert inhabit the deepness of the unlit wood. The wood-sorrel leaves are large, and darker now like all the other foliage. Where earlier in the year the floor was carpeted with garlic stars and bluebells, it is now littered with the yellow slimy debris of rotting leaves - out of which poke straight fleshy stems bearing seed pods, some of them breaking open to reveal shiny black seeds.

Everything seems to have reached the limit of its growth - the plants that have already produced seed are now letting their foliage die back. Towering grasses, no longer powdering pollen, are ripening to straw. All looks tired and spent - the freshest growth is of brambles and thistles.

A tall umbelliferae sticks its head above the undergrowth. I cannot get near enough to properly identify it, but guess it's hogweed.

If I were to bring only one piece of equipment here at this time of year, it would be my midge oil. A young robin watches me as I apply it liberally to all exposed skin. Out in the glade I see betony, where orchids grew last month, brightening the monotony of green. Clouds of flies swarm out of the bracken forest so I quickly retreat back into the gloom. They don't seem to bother the dog, whose fur is crawling with them, especially the black patches which will be warmer from absorbing the sunlight, whilst the white parts reflect it and stay cooler.

I cross the bridge and investigate the wild side. Low sun glints bronze and copper in the stream and a small trout darts into a shady crack as we pass. Bracken wraps itself around my legs and I have to crouch down to push through the dense mass of sloe and hazel. I struggle on until a nettlebed bars my passage. Not foolhardy enough to pursue that route, I return the way I came, listening to the jackdaws calling in the crags above and the young pheasants cackling together in the thicket below.

Perfectly matching the forest floor under the evergreens, the half-grown chicks cower motionless until we approach too close, and then stretch up their necks and run, zigzagging in bunches, running for better cover. Dappled light pierces the canopy, confusing the eye, shining intensely bright on groups of leaves, deepening the depths of the shadows.

I find St John's wort, with tight buds on branching stems, just coming into flower, next to wood burnett bearing little barbed burrs of seeds. The honeysuckle is still blooming, with more to come; and melancholy thistle's huge purple cushions attract the bees, whilst its relative, the knapweed, keeps tightly wrapped 'hardheads' until later in the year.

Daisy shows me a hedgehog's nest firmly lined with moss and hidden in the long grass. I don't want to disturb the contents but suspect there are babies there.

Along the fairy wood the deer are secretive, but have stripped leaves from the lower branches of the sycamore. Raspberries are formed but not yet ripe. Lords & ladies leaves are all gone; only sturdy stems remain, crowded with green berries..

Yellow vetch and lesser stitchwort climb together up the rough grass under the ash at the far top corner of the wood. We sit here, in the lee of the wall, watching the mature leaves turning up pale undersides as the wind blows billowing clouds over to the east.

A low-flying jet tears the sky apart. The flies do now annoy the dog, and she snaps and paws at them, impatient to be off again. I feel sad, knowing that I will not be able to get here again for a few weeks, and that the year is on the turn already. Next time, the end of year signals will be even stronger.

A pigeon's cooing soothes and comforts, and off we go to escape the flies. Back out into the windswept sunny dale, I see harebells, yarrow, and white clover growing along the meadow walls.

FRUITING

August

As I anticipated, the year
is on the turn, here in our
secret place. Today has been
a heavy, hazy August day.

The Dale is heaving with
holiday-makers. How I
appreciate being able to
escape up here to
solitude and peace.

The climb up to the
wood is through long
grass, juicy after a wet
summer. It is trodden down and
munched at by the cows, so I also have to watch where I walk! Turning
to look behind, I see dark blue distances and purple walls. Thundery
clouds cast indigo shadows on lush pastures.

Up at the boundary wall, the swaying foxglove spires bear mostly
seeds, but at their very summit an odd flower bell or two hangs on
still. Here a thriving population of craneflies swarms up,
disturbed by my tramping feet. Crimson hawthorn berries -
not yet the deep colour of ripeness, hang over the wall,
together with rosehips - some still green, some
turning to vermilion. Ash keys hang heavily,
weighing down the upturned branches.

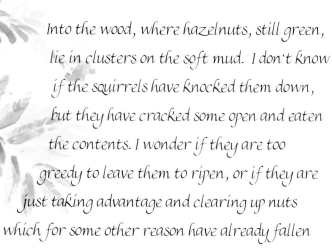

Into the wood, where hazelnuts, still green,
lie in clusters on the soft mud. I don't know
if the squirrels have knocked them down,
but they have cracked some open and eaten
the contents. I wonder if they are too
greedy to leave them to ripen, or if they are
just taking advantage and clearing up nuts
which for some other reason have already fallen
from the trees? Shafts of late afternoon light stretch across the glade where
another ancient hawthorn has fallen since my last visit, too tired to manage
another heavy fruiting season. Lichen has been growing ever more crusty and
thick over the hawthorn during each of its advancing years, and was already
covering more than eighty-per-cent of its branches and twigs.

Knapweed is in full magenta bloom among the graceful drying grasses of the
clearing. Scabious and self heal flower here too, but the melancholy thistle has
finished and hangs browned seed heads as if with exhaustion. The wet weather
has prevented the seed from fluffing out, like thistle tops should, to give the
wind a chance to blow them up and far away.

Ripe spores under the ferns make them look rusty, and the ten-foot tall bracken
is turning at the edges. There is no way at all through the thicket now; the ripe
raspberries are safe from me across the other side of the nettlebed.
There are black disease spots on the sycamore leaves. I read last year
that they are a sign of clean air - they are made by a fungus which
does not thrive where the air is polluted.

Sadly, I find across my path a large, dead hare; no reason for his death is apparent, but his eyes are now eaten out and the flies are enjoying his remains. Death is not always caused by misadventure - as with the hawthorn it could have been a natural end to a long life. Nothing will be wasted and the carcass will be cleared away long before the dead wood of the hawthorn disappears.

We continue our walk along the stream, its ever running flow confirming the deep connection I feel with the spiralling of life and death. Some yellowing leaves have already fallen into the whisky-coloured water - they are swirled away in the current. I stop to watch the midges dancing in a patch of sunlight and a rabbit quietly hops through in front of me, rattling the empty, papery bluebell seedcases as she passes. The alder leaves are old, a shiny tough dark green, scattered with blobs and blotches; but among the small upright cones hang stiff tight catkins for next year.

Blackbirds and thrushes feast upon ripe rowan berries up in the canopy; and in the undergrowth a colony of toadstools live off a pile of rotting branches. An old cock pheasant calls quietly, and a group of young birds scatter as we approach the bridge. Their adolescent plumage is already showing which are male and which female, but they still all call in childish squeaks and cheeps.

The bird cherry has once again
survived the voracious caterpillars,
and bears their cobweb sacks like
fruit amongst its twigs. There is not
much ground flora left under the
trees, but campion and herb robert
flower on in the odd dark corner,
whilst wood woundwort, looking leggy
and battered, perseveres.

Daisy plays the squirrel chasing game, and then runs from tree to tree, gazing
up with a tongue lolling grin. I call her back as we pass the young
pheasants again; and so, as we walk quietly together,
we startle the doe and half grown fawn from
their cover and watch them leap away into the
dappled darkness.

Later, even though the dead twigs are
crackling noisily under my feet, I'm very
glad to see a live and healthy hare start up
and escape into the nearby pasture.

Here, out of the wind, the evening turns hot and sultry,
and I am ready to climb out through the stile into the
hazy dale. Curlews call to the sunset and wood smoke
scents the air. Cows turned out from milking browse
their way through the 'follow on' grass of the meadow.
We stand and watch as man and dog, working together,
call up the cattle and open the gate for them so that they
may obediently meander through to pastures new.

September

The day is unfolding softly through a morning which began with a cold white fog swirling in the bottom of the dale. There is no sound from the rookery up there amongst the ageing foliage. Autumn hawkbit and yarrow decorate the pasture. We climb up out of the mists into crystal clarity, turning back as usual at the stile to survey the panorama laid out below. Every hollow is filled with drifting mist, in places so thick only the tips of trees stand out above it. The sun is warm and strong and soon the 'white ladies' will vanish away as silently as they came.

Our little utopia has a haze of its own, hanging over the stream and under the trees. Everything drips with morning dew, the bracken drooping heavily. Cobweb after cobweb, bejewelled with diamond drops, is slung across from grass to seed-head, from stem to low slung branch.

The brambles, late to develop, bear both flowers and hard green berries. Their neighbours are all well into fruiting and ripening: rosehips warm to vermilion and fatten into scarlet; the haws' crimson deepens; herb robert's crane's bills stand erect and blush, and wood burnett's burrs stick out hopeful of hooking into passing wool or fur.

Most of the rowan berries have already been devoured; they need to pass through the gut of hungry birds before being deposited somewhere else to wait for germination. The hazelnuts look a little more mature, but some still fall earlier than they should. Sloes, which flower first, are last to ripen. Dark and hard, they're green and difficult to see. Under the trees, the wood-sorrel leaves form a green baize covering where they have broadened and flattened out to collect all the sustenance they can from the light before the year cools.

Beneath the tunnel formed by overhanging branches, the amber stream flows on, reflecting back the blue above as the warming day clears through. We settle here to paint sun and shadow dappling over stone and water.

I am well into my work, absorbed into the problems of depicting wet stone and dry stone; stones at the bottom of the beck seen through the reflections on the surface; and the difference between fast flow and gentle eddy. Suddenly, I notice the dog's ears prick up as her attention is drawn to a movement downstream. Following her gaze I am thrilled by the sight of a heron flying upstream towards us. The arch of trees is too narrow for him to turn round or manoeuvre in any way at all - he has no option but to fly steadily on.

His silent flight, and great size, overawes us both, and all we can do is keep
stock still and watch his approach. The gap between us narrows to an arm's
length... a wing span.... and his wing-tip touches my easel as he passes, one
beautiful yellow eye looking straight into mine for magical seconds which seem
like lifetimes.

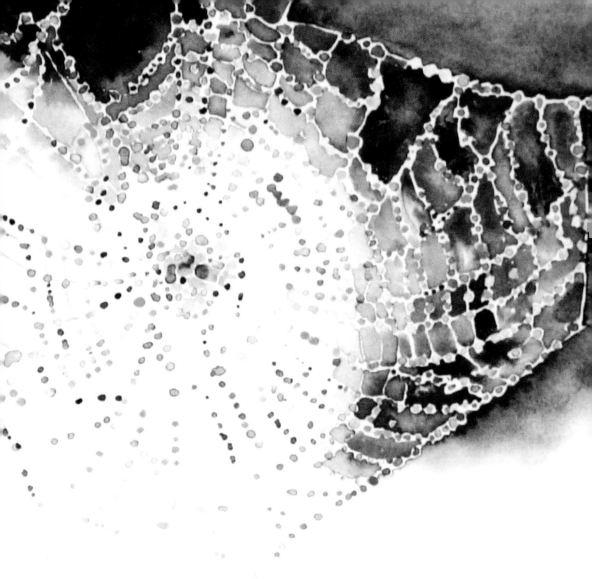

Having a break from work, midday, I scramble over wet rocks to climb the north slope where the sun is hot. It is deep and crisp below the holly where old leaves have been shed to make way for fresh new growth. We have had a late Indian summer, and the moss is dry and dusty again already, in spite of the dampness of the morning. Twigs crackle and snap under the pines and larches where young pheasants, with little fear, scratch and peck or dust-bathe. Spiders' webs, slung across from to twig to twig above me, now trawl the sunlight, which transforms them into rainbow nets.

I collapse on a dried out patch of grass, burnt umber and sienna ribbons, curling and twisting. In this little open space I am surrounded by fern and bracken and the buzzing of flies, leaving the midges to dance in the shadows under the heavy canopy. The topmost branches of an ash tree sway in a light breeze which does not reach the sweltering steamy valley, except to catch the fluffy thistle heads whose fairies fly off, up, and away... A tree creeper flits past with high pitched call, and a Hercules spider clambers over me, staggering on long gangly legs.

Back down below, the stream is slow and dark and cool, making pools of ripple and reflection. On this late summer, early autumn day, the wood seems to hang suspended in the space between lush growth and ripening harvest. A dragonfly flits a zigzag path over the water. The dog paddles in knee deep to drink, then lowers her belly and lies down in it to cool off!

Later, painting done, we leave the quiet murmuring of the wood pigeon and bubbling of the beck, and return home along the top of the south side. My shadow follows me, dragging reluctantly behind along the bottom of the valley.

Early October

I'm here early this morning. The rooks haven't left to forage yet and are busy, circling and calling amongst their sycamores, whose leaves are deepening to olive brown. The rosehips, vermilion and scarlet, shine- brilliant in a tapestry of ochre, green, and rusty orange foliage. Hazel nuts ripen, hanging pale warm brown from trees bedecked with leaves of acid yellow and lime green. Dark purple elderberries weigh down supple branches; these leaves are changing to a paler creamy yellow, though some elders can turn to a rich streaky crimson. The silver birches' tiny, brilliant yellow triangles spiral down to earth, where small orange fungi add to the kaleidoscope of colour. There are not enough words to describe the number of yellows I can see. I can paint them much more accurately than write them down.

Moist cobwebs tickle my face as I break through them on my way to the stream. I scratch my hands as I pick the glistening blackberries to supplement my breakfast. The beck tumbles on, as ever, now more the colour of sweet sherry. Caramel cream foam piles up between the rocks as it races past.

Then, what joy, as I stand and watch the movement of the water, a flash of electric blue dazzles past - the kingfisher...

Classic scarlet fly agaric, peppered with crusty white spots, have popped up under the silver birches - no dwarfs in sight! One of the stately birch trees, which had snapped in winter gales, now provides a habitat for a large bracket fungus. A scattering of puff-balls has been kicked over by a passing animal.

Tiny white toadstools, like pearl buttons, cluster in circlets under an ash.

Later, walking to the far end, I find even more fungi- a community of huge tan lactarius, tiny bonnet mycena and, on an old alder trunk, a stunning outcrop of sulphur tuft. Then, in a quiet corner where birch and holly grow together, a large ring of toadstools give off a pungent musty smell. Their wavy edges turn dark brown and putrid with age, the soft felty surface becomes a shiny slime to which fallen leaves stick, imprinting a textured pattern. I've had to give up trying to identify fungi. I learned enough to know what a specialised subject it is, and enough to make me very wary of handling them before eating my lunch.

The orchard hangs heavy with pendulous damsons. Closely related, the sloes did produce fruit, in spite of the late spring frost. Now, on prickly twigs clung with lichen, and sparkling with bright yellow leaves, they wait blue bloom high for an early autumn frost to juice them up before being picked for gin.

Homeward bound down the pasture in the clear warm dry evening air, I notice fluttering movements just above the surface of the field. Some small birds are feeding on the fully opened downy thistle-tops. They flit about collecting seed, fly up into the trees, then swoop back down again to feast.

I count twenty to
thirty of them...
the largest charm
of goldfinches I
have ever seen!

TURNING

Late October

We have had days and days of dull grey
rain, but last night was frosty and this
morning the sun rose into the day, like a
trumpet voluntary. The sky is blue from
horizon to horizon, and the low glittering
light glazes over a crisp white crystal
coating, quickly strengthening and
melting it away to reveal the richness of
full autumn glory. The canopy has turned
into a glorious riot of colour. A jewel of a
morning set stunningly in
a chain of murky days.

If the weather is wet, the
colours develop well, but without
sun to shine on the splendour, we
hardly notice the changes. Quiet, still
days with clear skies bring hard frosts
to wither up the leaves, killing them
before they have a chance to send
their precious goodness back into
the limbs and bodies of the trees;
too much wind whips away each
leaf as it changes colour.

High Close is inhabited by clean fresh dipped Swaledale ewes, developing a good healthy growth of wool to protect them through the winter. A Blue-faced Leicester ram, his chest dripping with 'ruddle', escorts them with an air of ownership. It's tupping time, and when he mounts each ewe as she becomes receptive, the stain on his underside rubs off on her backside, to tell the farmer who it was that fertilised her, and when - sowing seed for spring..

Hawthorne and rosehips glow against the coeruleum sky, a feast in store for the birds. Willow-herb seed pods, long and elegant, curl back and around, empty now of airy seed. Herb bennet, earthnut, and herb robert have completed their cycle of flowering and fruiting for another year. There is a self-satisfied feel to the wood - calm, mature, knowing that the job is done.

White hoar frost lingers in the valley bottom. I can hear the leaves gently snap themselves off the living twigs, pulled off by nothing more than their own weight. They float and flutter, twisting and turning, down ... down into the stillness where one by one they softly land onto the crunchy carpet of yellows, greens, browns, rusts, and deep, deep purples.

Unusually there is no sound from the beck, and I understand why when I get closer and see the rocks and water coated with fallen leaves. Underneath the thick covering, the stream gurgles gently and meanders from pool to pool. A moment ago I heard the deer bound across it and up the far side. I couldn't see them through the dazzling confusion of sharp sun and shadow of the tangled thicket, but find their hoof prints in the mud. Looking closely, I stumble and slip, discovering that a deceptively dry carpet of leaves is, in fact, afloat on a deep still pool - water up to my ankles!

It is impossible to move quietly in the wood today - the scrunching of my boots through the deep layer of leaves betrays my presence. I am unable to move forwards without breaking through the intricate nets of gossamer that glisten in the sun.

We do see the young pheasants scatter at our approach, and I keep Daisy by me - away from the temptation to chase. Standing still, I hear the soft chuck-chuck of a blackbird in the holly, and the calling of the rooks passing high above me. Then, just when I think that I won't see much today, a tiny wren in the undergrowth delights me, so secretive in its habits - flitting with quick small movements.

The bracken, as it dies back, turns from green through pale ochre to rust, but where frost has caught, it has copper and pewter hues. In the shady places, ferns weaken to a pallid luminescence. Grasses bleach out, curling to calico ribbons as they dry. Golden larches, a startling colour, their tips feathery, sway into the blue - an unbelievable, unpaintable contrast; a transient dazzling shock of orange against an infinity of sky. Birches sparkle, scattering clear yellow. Hazels whisper a softer but acid ochre, in the intimacy of dark down to earth...

- the last fling of glory before battening down for winter.

I gather ripened sloes into my hat from lichen crusted twigs, and the sun lowers gently, chilling the afternoon air.

November

All the leaves are gone from the sycamores, and the rookery is exposed.
The rooks are all out and away today, a sunny and mild morning after days of
dowly drizzle, and cold winds. The oaks still hang on to some of their thinning
rusty canopy.

The pasture is a dull green, and a livid purple cloud hangs above the crag behind.
Ewes, their bottoms bedecked with red, yellow or blue, huddle together as the
wind gets chillier. Their tup boasts a yellow-green stain on his chest - colour of
the week.

In the wood the wind has whipped most of the leaves away, stripping
the twigs, which now reach, bare, up to the sky. Ash trees already
show next year's hard ebony buds, as this year's leaves rot to inky
black below. The carpet of colour is now bedding down to form a rich
brown slime to protect the roots and shoots from winter frosts.
Darkening leaves shine wet mauve, reflecting the sky above.

The hazel twigs, now bereft of yellow leaves, carry tiny
awkward catkins. Lichens and mosses come into their own,
creeping and clinging to everything. Bracken collapses,
bedraggled in weak sunshine. Occasionally a bird cheeps, but
otherwise in the woodland all is quiet.

The sun is low all day. On the southside of the valley it
only touches the topmost twigs of the trees, forming a
slanting line of sun and shadow on the grey green
trunks and mostly leafless branches.

Everything is dripping, and in the stream some late fallen leaves are caught up in the current. They float down, rapidly twisting and bobbing, before pausing in slower water at the foot of an alder. In the deep pool the yellow leaves sink, rise, and turn languidly, down and out of sight into the peaty blackness. Floating back up into view on the bubbled surface, they swim aimlessly round and round... then, suddenly caught in an eddy, they dance like whirling dervishes before being flung back into the mainstream where they are swept along and away.

A branch, cast down during the recent windstorm, is stuck across the beck, trapped by the tumbled rocks. The leaves and bubbles are caught here, and collect together to form piles of foam, whipped cream mountains on a shaking jelly.

Emerging from the wood, I turn to look behind me. The tops of the larches are still an impressive sight, though now dulled to a tawny orange; in the low sun.

Late November

A blanket of fog crept stealthily up
the dale overnight to make the day even
darker and shorter. A fine drizzle cools my face
as I walk up the hill to the wood. The rooks call to
each other in the gloom - short intimate croaks as
they sit in pairs in their sycamores. I can hear a steady
drip, drip, dripping all around me as moisture gathers
itself into drops of sufficient weight to fall down onto
the wet rotting leaves. There is a heaviness in the
earth, muddy and sploshy; it seems to wait, holding
its breath again at the end of a season...

The purple and green haze of branches and twigs is
enriched here and there by a mass of crimson
hawthorn berries as yet uneaten. Some of the oak
leaves still hang on - the frosts came before the
nutrients had fully drawn back into the body of
the tree, halting the natural progression of
turn and fall. A dead elm, moss and lichen
clinging to its twigless branches, has fallen
across the stream. Mosses thicken up
everywhere, revelling in the cold damp,
creeping insidiously over everything.

I cannot stay out and paint for long
today, the cold settles into my bones and the
steady drips have found a way down the back of my
neck to complete my chilling. I set my thoughts on home to
the warmth and light of our fireside.

Holly shines dark gloss, berries glowing scarlet. Their growth is so
slow it is a miracle to me that the holly trees still survive when we
take so much of it for our seasonal celebrations. Nature only takes
what it needs from itself, but we get greedy about something for which
we have no real need. However, this year they are laden with berries.
The farmer's wife tells me she's never seen so many.

Christmas will be well decorated.

The smell of smoke from the village chimneys lingers in the air.

SLEEP

December

Mist hangs low in the valley and my
world is powdered everywhere with a fine
white rime. As I walk up across the fields,
my feet make a quiet crunching sound, as
they flatten the frozen grass blades.

The sun, rising above the
edge of the fell, bathes what it
touches with a warm primrose
light, throwing long blue shadows of
the trees over the gentle curves of the
sleeping earth. In this light the cold
white coating sparkles, an
encrustation of tiny jewels spread,
grown and crystallised by last night's
freezing fog; the deathly pallor of the
frost turned to shining
diamonds by the sun.

Coated with velvet mosses, the trunks and lower limbs glow sap and olive greens, reaching out of the dark silence of the wood. Higher, the twigs and branches reflect rich warm tones of bronze and ochre on clear coeruleum where windswept leaves stubbornly cling on. Holly and ivy, in their prime, contrast strongly with the nakedness of their neighbours. Holly, sturdy and ancient, bears Christmas berries shining bright. Dense ivy sends out star like explosions of flower buds, as it drapes tenaciously over a strangled ash.

Yesterday's tracks in soft and sloppy mud, are today turned to imprints of stone. The low sun strikes through the trees making it difficult to see beyond to the deep cold gully of the stream.

Too soon the light begins to dim, the shadows lengthen even more, and the air takes on the bitterness of encroaching nightfall, although the clock says only afternoon. Midwinter days are so short. Mother used to call these 'the dark days before Christmas'...

New Year

We had a snowfall overnight - I waded
here through deep drifts. As I approached
the boundary wall a woodcock flew out;
then, startled by my approach, he
quickly zigzagged back into the trees.

Snow blankets all - a miracle of white. Silence prevails.

Under all this wonderland, I know that the sap will soon be
stirring; the sleeping does not last forever. Branches lie on the
ground like skeletons, once more stripped of bark. The animals
have desperately gnawed at anything they could get to see them
through the lean times. But branches overhead, though stuck with snow,
are bearing secret packages of potential growth. Leaf buds, tightly wrapped, and
short hard catkins, built to survive the icy blasts, simply wait.

As I paint, the snow is slightly warmed and begins to slip quietly off the trees, dimpling the pristine surface below. The whole wood has slowly begun to stir, to move a little in its sleep...

as if my thoughts had permeated through, and connected with the subconscious
of the dreamer, as it begins to take deeper breaths - a prelude to waking...

Guide to the illustrations

Generally the descriptions are from left to right and top to bottom

Page

4	tortoiseshell butterfly
5	primroses and wood sorrel
8 & 9	immature hazel catkins, old hawthorn berries, lichens and moss, sloe - twigs and buds, hazelnut shells opened by squirrel and woodmouse, dead bracken
10 & 11	lichens & mosses
12 & 13	hazel catkins, willow, alder - immature catkins and cones, honeysuckle leaves, hawthorn, moss
14	snowdrops, ivy, mosses and lichens
15	hazel catkins - male and female flowers, pussy willow
16 & 17	rooks & sycamores
18 & 19	flowers of willow and larch; flower buds of rowan; buds and sprouting leaves of willow, sycamore, larch, wild rose, rowan, hazel, hawthorn; and long tailed tits
20	rosettes of bluebell, foxglove, the first primrose, celandine
21	daffodils & coltsfoot flowering with emerging garlic leaves
22 & 23	hare
24	Swaledale ewe and lamb
25	herb-paris, dogs mercury, garlic, primrose
26	fern, celandine
27	pheasant
28	sycamore, rowan, ash
29	bird cherry, willow, hawthorn
30	stoat
31	fern, primrose, wood sorrel, celandine, barren strawberry, common dog violet
34	pussy willow
35	fern. dogs mercury, herb paris, milkmaid (ladies smock or cuckoo flower), garlic buds, bluebell, primrose, false oxlip, cowslip, early purple orchid, violet, wood forget-me-not, wood speedwell
36	early purple orchid, bluebell, sanicle, goldilocks, wood anemone, bugle, wild barren strawberry, yellow pimpernel
39	sloe blossom, sycamore unfolding leaves, blackberry leaves
40	bird cherry
41	hare
42	peacock butterflies
43	bluebells and garlic (ramsons)
44	goldilocks, woodruff, stitchwort, wood anemone, moschatel, golden saxifrage
45	fern, bracken
46	fresian cows
47	fern, lords & ladies, water aven, earth nut (Queen Annes lace or pignut)
48 & 49	clockwise from top left: sycamore, ash, oak, alder, elder, hazel, downy birch, grey willow, honeysuckle, wild rose, hawthorn, sloe, rowan, bird cherry

50	hedgehog
51	roe deer
52 & 53	unfurling bracken
55	fox
56	red admiral
57	foxglove, fern, herb bennet (wood avens), red campion
60	pied wagtail
62	ferns
63	roe deer
64	elder in flower
65	honeysuckle, wild rose
66	yorkshire fog
67	trout
69	hedge woundwort, nipplewort, perforate St Johns wort, betony, herb robert, broad leaved willow herb
70 & 71	clockwise from top left: fruits of: ash, sycamore, sessile oak, hazel, alder
72 & 73	rowan berries, blackbird, song thrush
74	grey squirrel
75	curlew
77	hazel nuts
78 & 79	heron
81	blackberries
82	kingfisher
83	haws (hawthorn), sloes (blackthorn), dog rose hips, damsons, elderberries, rowan berries, blackberries, soft downy rose hips
84	birch
85	fungi: sulphur tuft, fly agaric, and (possibly) several milk-caps (lactarius), a russula, and some mycena
86 & 87	goldfinches and thistle seeds
88 & 89	clockwise from top left: birch, sycamore, …, wild cherry, hazel, hawthorn, …, sycamore, wych elm, sycamore, ash, alder, hazel, wild cherry
90	roe deer
92	larches
93	bracken
96 & 97	brittle bladder fern, mosses, lichens, birch leaves
102	holly
103	holly, fir and fir cones, Japanese larch cones, ivy

The cover, and illustrations on pages 58 & 59, and 106 & 107 are the same view across the flat glade in spring, summer, and winter respectively

The hardback edition has endpapers consisting of twelve paintings, one for each month of the year, of the same patch of ground under a hazel tree. Comparing the development of the ground cover throughout the twelve month period shows clearly how early the plants flower before the canopy cuts out the light

subscribers

Christine Adams	Betty Buttrick	Peter & Dorcas Downs	Ian Christopher Harland
Gilly Aitken	Noreen Byrne	Ted Downs	J Harran
Brian Alderson		Margaret Drinkell	Ann Harriman
Mr P C J Andrew	Mary Callaway	Sheila Dyde	Cerina Harris
Digby Angus	A Calvert	Jeremy Dyson	John Harris
Joan Angus	Jim Cannell		Jacqueline Hart
Angela K. Appleyard	Valerie Cannon	David Edward	Diane & Gerald Haughton
Frances Mary Atkinson	Heather Caplin	Martin Eland	Rosamund Haw
Mary Elizabeth Atkinson	Barbara Carne	Dr. Richard Ellis	Pat Heath
Shawn L. Auble	N A Carruthers	John Barry Emmett	Mary Heathcote
Jean Ayers	Andrew G. Casewell	Kate Empsall	Mary Hellawell
	Joyce Challis	Edna Entwistle	K E Hewson
E M Baker	Irene Cheeseman		Tony Hickson
Mrs Trish Baker	Peter & Pauline Chevins	Carol Few	Mabel Hilliar
Stephan Ball	Margaret Clark	Catherine Fewlass	Maureen A Hird
Eileen Bannister	Mary Clark	E. Fisher	Maggie Hoban
J M Barclay	Ann Clarke	S Fisher	Winifred Hodge
Val Barker	Jacqueline Avril Clarkson-Jones	Charles A. Fletcher	Ann Holubecki
Edna & Raymond Barnard	Brian Clement	Maureen Fletcher	Janina Holubecki
Mollie Barstow	Barbara Clements	Susan Foster	Marysia Holubecki
W T Bates	David Trevose Clowe	J. Fulton	Kate Hooper
Sheilah Beningfield Collis	Susan Cochrane	Mattie Furnish	Josephine Hopper
Chris & Terry Bell	Eileen Cockburn	Sue Francis	Elsie E Hornsey
Stephen & Gladys Bent	Andrea Cockerill		Don Horton
Jean Bird	Margaret Codling	D P Game	Norma Horton
Sheila Black	Chris Considine	P Gardam	Marion Hoyle
Florence Bland	Caroline Coode	Alexandra C. Gatty	Tony M. Hughes
Dian Blawer	S Costigan	Deborah Gentry	Benjamin Hussey
June M Boardall	Henry Cotton	D J Giddens	
Roelof & Anne Boersma	John Cousens	Sarah Gillette	Margaret Iveson
Paula Bowers	J E Crabtree	Ruth Godsell	
Barbara Bowling	W Crabtree	Rita Goldhawk	Dave & Jenny Jackson
Marie Brandeth	Dorothy Cradock	Avril D. Golding	Mrs Freda Jackson
Sheila and Tony Bratton	John Creedon	David & Margaret Gray	Judith Jackson
Penelope Bray	Norma Croft	Mrs Mary Gray	Julie Jennings
Peter Charles Brears	Audrey Culling	Catherine Green	Bryan Johnson
J R Bridgford		Eleanor Greenstreet	Lynette Johnson
Frank Brimmell	Jenny Dabbs	Kathy Groom	Jean Johnston
Dora Bromley	A J Davey		Hazel Jones
Peter Brooks	Dorothy Dawson	Joan Hackman	J V Joyce
D R Brown	Dorothy Day	E Hall	
Kate Brown	Anne Deans	L A Halpern	Agnes Kane
Sheila Burnham	Edith Dobson	Martin Hanson	M W Keys
	Ian Dormor	M Hardman	Grace Kingsley

John Kirby

C Knightley

Barbara Lambert

Rev. D H & Mrs B Lambert

Diana Lampen

Alan Landsell

Daphne Lanham

Anne Laurence

Kate Lawrence

Mike & Elizabeth Leake

Kay Lee

Vivien Leigh

David Lewis

Sheila Liddle

Steven Liddle

Margot Lomax

Howard Loughlin

J Lowbridge

H Lyons

M Macgregor

Jane Macintosh

Maureen & Dave Malyon

Dorothy Maney

Kingston & Anne Marflitt

Winnie Mark

Brenda Marsden

J. Marsden

Richard Maskrey

Ruth Maxwell

Margaret Joyes Mayell

Michael McAskie

Ann & Ian McLean

Sue McNicol

Susan Mencer

Janet Messent

Derek Mills

Jeannie Mills

Joy Milton

Leslie Douglas Minns

W Moran

Helen Morrison

Gwen Moss

Karen Mountain

Rosalind Muir

Jean Murphy

Gary & Clare Murrell

Mr Gordon Naylor

Miriam Nicholson

Joan OConnor

Valerie OConnor

Ruth Ogden

Sybil M Ogden

Margaret Overend

R Oxtoby

Clive Parker

David & Jean Parkes

Jane Parkinson

Valerie Payne

Anne Pearson

Diana Edith Penn

Beryl Percival

Zeta Perkins

Gerard Petiot

Robert Petty

Anne Picot

Gillian Pike

Christine Pill

Wendy Platt

Anne Povey

P R E Procter

Mrs D M Proctor

M J Powers

S Purcell

S Ralph

A N Reed

D Reed

Pat Reed

M & J Reffitt

Gwen Renton

Pam Rhodes

Susan Rhodes

Julia Ridley

Martin Robertson

Derrick Robinson

Rose Romani

Margaret Rooker

Niki Ropner

Janet Rudd

Edna Saul

Barry Sampson

Muriel Sawtell

Margaret H. Scarr

Cyril Schofield

Janice Serginson

Joan Sharpe

Charles & Alison Shaw

John & Barbara Shaw

John Sheard

Margaret Shepperd

Pat Skidmore

K.E. & M. I. Smallpage

Audrey Smith

Cilla & Chris Smith

Mavis Smith

William J.T.Smith

Timothy Solloway

Robert Southall

Angie Spray

L Stevens

W Steventon

Anne Stimson

John & Brenda Stirling

David & Lynne Stott

Roger Stott

Peter Sutcliffe

N Taylor

Patricia Taylor

Verena Thirkettle

Alison Thompson

Vicki Thompson

Lorna Thornborrow

Karen Thorne

Kevin & Alison Thwaites

Lois & Derek Thwaites

Jennifer Tole

N Tungate

M & I Turnbull

Jack Turner

Annie Uden

Dorothy Utting

Michael & Hazel Waldman

Ella Walker

David Wall

M A Walton

Mike & Pat Walton

Christine Webb

E Webb

Jan Webb

Eric and Barbara Webster

Sylvia Western

Michael J. Westgate

Jeanne White

Joan Whitmarsh

J B Whyley

J & S Wiley

R Willetts

Florence Williams

Karen Williams

Helen Willis

Jean Wilson

John R Winter

Roy Woodhead

Margery Woods

Susan Woods

Freda Woodyer

Phil Woodyer

Nicholas Worsley

Dorothea Worsley-Taylor

Albert & Brenda Wright

M Wright

Billie J Wylie

Judy Yielder

Kim Youd

Anne Young

Pippa Young